# The BOOK of WAKING DREAMS

## Stories of the Dream Man

Gerald L. Kovacich

authorHOUSE®

AuthorHouse™
1663 Liberty Drive
Bloomington, IN 47403
www.authorhouse.com
Phone: 1 (800) 839-8640

© 2015 Gerald L. Kovacich. All rights reserved.

No part of this book may be reproduced, stored in a retrieval system, or transmitted by any means without the written permission of the author.

Published by AuthorHouse 04/27/2015

ISBN: 978-1-5049-0370-7 (sc)
ISBN: 978-1-5049-0371-4 (e)

Library of Congress Control Number: 2015904918

Print information available on the last page.

Any people depicted in stock imagery provided by Thinkstock are models, and such images are being used for illustrative purposes only.
Certain stock imagery © Thinkstock.

This book is printed on acid-free paper.

Because of the dynamic nature of the Internet, any web addresses or links contained in this book may have changed since publication and may no longer be valid. The views expressed in this work are solely those of the author and do not necessarily reflect the views of the publisher, and the publisher hereby disclaims any responsibility for them.

The book's cover provided by Mike of Bandana's Skin Art, 2603 Commercial Ave., Anacortes, WA, 98221; Email: bandana@me.com; Telephone: 360-299-9831.

## *Dedication*

### To Dreamers

May your dreams bring you meaning and guide you to the Tao[1].

Om mani padme hum[2]

---

[1] The absolute principle underlying the universe, combining within itself the principles of yin and yang and signifying the Way, or code of behavior, that is in harmony with the natural order (New Oxford American Dictionary, Oxford University Press, 2001).

[2] **14th Dalai Lama**
"It is very good to recite the mantra Om mani padme hum, but while you are doing it, you should be thinking on its meaning, for the meaning of the six syllables is great and vast... The first, Om [...] symbolizes the practitioner's impure body, speech, and mind; it also symbolizes the pure exalted body, speech, and mind of a Buddha[...]"
"The path is indicated by the next four syllables. Mani, meaning jewel, symbolizes the factors of method: (the) altruistic intention to become enlightened, compassion, and love.[...]"
"The two syllables, padme, meaning lotus, symbolize wisdom[...]"
"Purity must be achieved by an indivisible unity of method and wisdom, symbolized by the final syllable hum, which indicates indivisibility[...]"
"Thus the six syllables, om mani padme hum, mean that in dependence on the practice of a path which is an indivisible union of method and wisdom, you can transform your impure body, speech, and mind into the pure exalted body, speech, and mind of a Buddha[...]"
(Wikipedia)

# Preface

Did you ever have a waking dream? In other words, you were somewhere between awake and asleep, or maybe a dream, or nightmare that was so real that you felt all that was in the dream or you were not really dreaming? You felt all the pain, stress, joy, sadness – all the human emotions that were part of that dream? Strange dreams that made no sense at all or some making some sense to you or to others you told?

Did you consider that maybe you were given that dream so you could learn from it or didn't give it much thought? Have you ever thought that maybe your dreams, especially the more of a waking dream, the more detailed and vivid of your dreams, were maybe your past lives' experiences intruding on this life, or what you should do in the future in this life? Maybe there was a message in your dreams that you were to not only learn from, but also there to tell you to take or not take certain actions?

Have you ever had a recurring dream? One that seemed to come back in your waking sleep-dream state time after time, or at least some version of it? If so, what did you do about it? Do your dreams have patterns, recurring themes or were they few and far in between, and never were repeated?

Try this: place a pad of paper and a pen near your bed. The next time you dream, try very hard to remember it. As soon as you awake, immediately write it down. Don't wait thinking you will remember it in the morning since you probably won't, or at least not in the detail maybe you could if you had immediately written it down. You may have a difficult time at first but hopefully, you will eventually get the experience, the discipline necessary to write down your dreams in detail, in your "dream diary". After a while maybe you could find patterns, themes that run through your various dreams, analyze them and determine their meanings.

I believe we dream for a reason. We dream about our past lives as our lives are not just the one we are living but include past lives that make up who we are now. We are multi-dimensional beings and that means in time, space and more than three-dimensional also, but few humans appreciate that part of us or even realize it. We are a collection of all that came before us, inherited in the genes and the experiences of our ancestors, in our past lives, in our current life. All of that prepares us for our lives yet to come.

This book is a work of fiction but based on dreams of all sorts and nightmares of people who have told me their stories. I used those "kernels" of their stories to tell the tale of an old man who collects various dreams and nightmares of others, interprets their dreams, works with their Karma; and impacts and changes the lives of the dreamers. Most of his receipt of dreams come in that state between awake and asleep, called the "waking dreams state". That is the only way the Dream Man can describe it. He has never actually had his own dreams as other humans have had. He is an unusual human being and the last of his clan.

By the way, who is to say there is no such being, human or otherwise?

# Introduction

The Dream Man is himself literally a dreamer, a constant dreamer. However, he is a different sort of dreamer as he collects or "dreams" the dreams of others and not his own. He has no choice. Although never having had a personal dream, he tries not to collect dreams at all but he cannot stop. It is his destiny, his Karma in this life to collect the dreams of others.

No matter whether they are a collection of the dreams of other humans, maybe even other life forms, or a combination of all that, he must "absorb" them and then decide what to do about them.

He, being a Tibetan Buddhist, finds it easiest to classify his collected dreams as either yin, yang, or yin-yang dreams. In other words, they are either good dreams, bad dreams or a combination of both. After all, such are the emotions of the human dreamers. All of life's emotions can be divided into some good, some bad or some in-between emotions and thus, so can dreams be categorized. Of course, as would anyone, he dreads the bad dreams and prefers the good ones. However, if he had a choice of course he would prefer not dreaming at all.

His Karma is to interpret the dreams that he absorbs. He is sometimes that little voice that you may hear when you are in a dream-state, in meditation or otherwise in a quiet-mind state.

Why? He doesn't know why but he does know that he must and by doing so fulfill his destiny and maybe provide dreams' replies, or direction or nudges to send the dreamers in certain directions that help them, to guide them in the right direction down their right path in life, to the Tao with all its mysteries, illusions, and code of behavior that guides each of us to be in harmony with the natural order of the universe. Sometimes though it is to stop the dreamers' current behavior which is creating bad Karma.

This book incorporates some of his waking dreams' stories. What you the reader think of them, well that is up to you to interpret, to ignore, to learn from his waking dreams. Maybe only one will hit a chord with you; maybe that one is all you need, maybe none will, maybe more than one.

Maybe that is all that is needed and the old man's use of a particular dream or dreams will help him fulfill his destiny so that he soon can literally rest in peace, and thus, send him on his way, to where we know not – at least not until the end of the book.

# Acknowledgments

I must acknowledge the role that my Karma has played in my life, leading me, sometimes kicking and screaming to the right path that is leading me to the Tao.

Also thanks to so many others that have played a role and influence in my life for decades. The many Buddhist monks and other Buddhists that I have had the pleasure of knowing and gaining insight through conversations with them in China, to include Taiwan and Tibet; as well as Cambodia, Thailand, and Japan. They have given me insight into life and the philosophy and joy of showing compassion, patience, love and charity to all sentient beings – all of which have changed my life for the better.

This book could never have been published without the support and dedication of the most brilliant freelance editor I have had the pleasure of working with for over 15 years, Sandy Nichol, to whom I owe a special thanks.

A special thanks also to Mike of Bandana's Skin Art, 2603 Commercial Ave., Anacortes, WA, 98221; Email: bandana@me.com; Telephone: 360-299-9831, for providing his great art work that is used for this book's cover. A special thanks also for giving me the best tattoos a person could ever ask for! Thanks Dude!

Thanks also to all those who have over the years shared their often intimate, personal dreams with me. They are male, female, young, old and in-between. They come from a multitude of different backgrounds, cultures, races, colors and creeds. They all have dreamt as that human trait knows no prejudices.

Thanks to all!

# Contents

Preface ................................................................................... vii
Introduction ............................................................................ xi
Acknowledgments ................................................................. xiii

**I  History of the Dream Man** ............................................... 1
In the Void .............................................................................. 3
Introduction to the Dream Man ............................................. 5
And Then There Was One ...................................................... 9

**II  Stories of the Collected Dreams of the Dream Man** ....... 13
The Lesson of the Fish .......................................................... 15
What Goes Around, Comes Around ..................................... 18
The Keys ............................................................................... 22
His Significant, Emotional Event .......................................... 25
The Hummingbird ................................................................. 30
First Came the Children and the Birds Then Came Death .... 32
Shattered Life Like Shattered Glass ..................................... 35
The Promise .......................................................................... 38
Happy Birthday From Mom .................................................. 42
The Spiders .......................................................................... 46
The Little Girl Who Defeated "The Evil One" ....................... 49

Young Heart, Old Soul ................................................................ 52
Books Don't Bring Enlightenment ............................................... 60
Better Late Than Never ............................................................. 64
Bear the Guardian ..................................................................... 66
Help Me! I Want to Fall ............................................................ 69
Daddy's Ring ............................................................................ 72

**III  The End is Near** ................................................................ 75
The Death Dream ...................................................................... 77
Return to the Void .................................................................... 79

**IV  Final Comments** ............................................................... 81

About the Author ..................................................................... 83

# HISTORY OF THE DREAM MAN

# IN THE VOID

What happens when we die is the greatest mystery of mysteries. Prior to being born, the Dream Man found that he, like other spirits or souls, remain alive, awaiting reincarnation in a place he called the Void.

"Where am I?" the child asked in the stillness of the dark.
"You are in the Void," said the Voice gently, almost in a whisper.
"What is the Void?" asked the child.
"It is the place of rest for souls between lives."
"I can't see. Why can't I see?"
"Because you have no eyes," replied the Voice.
"Why can't I feel anything?" the child asked.
"Because you are in spirit only and without physical substance," the Voice said.
"What will become of me?" asked the child.
"You will be reborn," said the Voice.
"Reborn? You mean I was born before?" the child asked.
"Yes," said the Voice, "many times."
"When will I be reborn?" asked the child.
"When your time has come," the Voice answered.
"What is the purpose of being reborn?"

The Voice answered, "For your soul to continue to learn and to give love."

"I don't understand," said the child.

"You ask many questions," the voice replied.

"I'm sorry," the child said, "is that wrong?"

"No, it is not wrong, it shows that you want to learn. That is a good sign," the Voice answered with a tone that comes between a laugh and a smile. "You will be returning soon, be patient," said the Voice.

"Who will I be?" the child asked.

The Voice said, "You will be known as the Dream Man. Enough talk. Meditate as your time for rebirth is coming soon and you will have a special task to perform upon rebirth."

"What special task?" asked the child.

"Now you are asking too many questions. Meditate as your time is near," answered the Voice.

# Introduction to the Dream Man

> Some special people are destined to be a vessel of others' dreams, whether they like it or not. The person called the "Dream Man" is one such unique person.

The old man sat up in bed as if propelled by a powerful, unseen force; being jolted from his sleep, and again feeling hot, again dripping in sweat, his heart beating so loud and fast, he swore he could hear it echoing off the walls of his cave. "Not again! Not again!" he cried out but no one was there to hear him. "I will soon go mad if this does not stop!" he yelled to no one. "Why can't I just sleep? Why must I dream, dream such dreams, waking dreams, nightmares worst of all? This makes no sense to me!" And yet, he knew his denial was false. He knew what they meant.

The old man called them "waking dreams" because they were so vivid, so real, he felt all that he dreamt – the pain, the stress, everything – as if he was not dreaming and yet he knew he was not really awake either, maybe in that in-between state. What bothered him the most though was that these dreams were not his, they came from some unknown place and yet, they always found him.

Suddenly, he heard the Voice say, "Because". Was that voice part of a dream? It sounded familiar. Yes, he knew he had heard it before but could not remember when, where or was he yet dreaming? No, not just a voice, but a voice that seemed to come from within and yet, a voice that boomed so loud as if it were coming from the walls of his cave itself. A familiar voice that came to him. One that he has heard as far back as he can remember. He heard it time and time and time again.

Please God, Lord Buddha, or whoever or whatever you are! Please let me die, let me die now," said the old man. "All those I loved are long gone, and I am left behind. I am so old, so tired. Please, please take me now, let me finally sleep, sleep without dreaming."

"No!" the Voice answered. "No, not until you have learned. Not until you complete your life – complete what you are here to do."

"I don't understand," said the old man.

"You will! Someday you will. Look within yourself. You know what you must do; you always knew what you must do and you also know why!" the Voice replied becoming somewhat irritated since the old man had been complaining for over 300 years.

The old man did know, at least he always felt he knew why he was here. Why he drew breath, but he grew selfish as he grew old. He neglected the work. He neglected his reason for being, for being in this life, in this time, but then again, he always fought his destiny.

Everything he had done in his life up to now was what he had to do to reach this final stage, this final experience in learning and not only learning but practicing what he had learned so that he could move on to the next life. For if he did not learn and practice what he had learned, he would not move on in the next life but move backward once again, as he had done thousands of times before when he fought his destiny, his Karma. Fought it to his last breath. He knew he must collect, interpret and send back thoughts, dreams, decide to influence or not influence the Karma of others.

He was raised in Western Tibet by a devout Buddhist mother. He came from a family of waking dreamers who for centuries collected, interpreted and shared their dreams' interpretations with all who were destined to learn from their interpretations, their dream influences. But he thought he was different. He wanted to be different, but only different from his family. He wanted to be like everyone else. He wanted to be ordinary so he fought the receipt of waking dreams. He fought them for several centuries but to no avail. They came and they came often, especially after the death of his mother.

He knew he had to do what his inner voice told him to do as he had no choice; he was the instrument commanded by some power beyond his comprehension. Finally, he surrendered to that unknown power. He could no longer ignore his destiny, his reason for being.

So, he collected the dreams of others. He then did what that inner voice in his waking dream state told him to do. He did so every day, at all hours of the day and night. He complied with his inner voice, hoping the dreams would stop and his life could stop, but he hated his waking dreams state and every day wished it would end forever.

His waking dreams state continued and he believed it would continue until humans no longer dreamed, until they no longer needed their dreams to lead them on their path in this life; until they were able to learn to listen, to interpret their own dreams and surrender to their dreams so that their dreams could guide them on the right path, to take the Middle Way of their lives; the path of Tao, all without his help.

But he also held out hope that eventually someone else would take his place so his mind – no, his very soul – could finally be at peace. So he continued in his waking dreams state as he entered his third century of life, at least his current life.

# AND THEN THERE WAS ONE

One of the Dream Man's worst memories was what he had been told to him by his mother when he was very young, and yet he also perceived the story of the last days of his ancestors. It was about his birth, their deaths and the destruction of his clan, leaving only him and his mother, and then only him.

It was Spring when it was about to turn into that time of calving of the yaks. His great-grandfather sat on a small rise, outside his yurt, meditating and enjoying the sun's wonderful bounty of its rays shining down on his old bones and warming them better than any winter yurt fires ever could; watching his pregnant granddaughter and his clan members working in the fields. It was one of Tibet's glorious days of pure air, pure water in the streams, the barley grasses of the plains were waving in the soft, body-caressing, warm summer breeze. It sounded what he thought the ocean waves would sound like although he had never actually heard them as Western Tibet is located far from any ocean.

In the far horizon stood those magnificent Himalayas crowned by that grand goddess of them all – Mt Everest or Chomolungma (Holy

Mother) as they called her; the barley bending in the breeze as if bowing to the Holy Mother so far away.

There was a peace that could only be known by a man at peace in this world of suffering. A silence broken only by the wind in the barley fields, the song of birds, and the noise of the yaks grazing in the fields and also broken on occasion by the laughter and yelling of his clan members, their children, tending the herds with their large mastiffs occasionally barking out a command to wolves waiting in the hills, telling them to stay away.

Surely if there was a Nirvana on earth, this was it, he thought. Then he heard it, slowly at first, then growing louder, the sounds of yelling, of machines moving, grinding Mother Earth. As it grew louder, he saw them coming, coming like a plague of locusts, eating everything in their sight, but in this case it was the tracks of men-carriers, of tanks grinding to death the yaks, the barley; and then the shooting started from these riding and walking locusts. Plowing through the fields, slaughtering everything they could see, be it yak, barley plant, dogs, and worst of all, his clan.

The old man sat there in shock, not able to move except the movement of tears dripping down his face which flowed like the river before him. He sat that way for what seemed days, although it was less than a few minutes. He had not been able to move, not even fathom what happened. He was in shock, total horrible shock. He turned and vomited until there was nothing left to vomit.

Then he stood up and screamed as only a human soul tortured and in shock could scream. The scream that comes from way within, the place usually protected where the body tries to defend itself from the horrors of the suffering on this earth. He screamed to the gods who certainly heard him as his tortuous screams echoed throughout the plains. He screamed to the Holy Mother too. He ran to stop them but he too was cut down by the machines of death. They ground through them, never stopping, ever-destroying, moving on until they were over the far horizon.

When they were gone and silence returned to the fields followed only by the noise and the movement of the vultures – those beasts that were Nature's way of cleaning up the messes made by humans. However, there was also another movement, and then a scream. It was not the bullet wound that had grazed her head rendering her initially unconscious that caused her to scream, but the screams of one soon to be become a mother. The screams of a woman giving birth which at the same time, woke her from her unconscious state as if Nature was saying, now is no time to sleep, now is the time to replenish the cycle of human life. To give birth to a special one to carry on the clan's heritage, their gift to other humans.

And so, he was born, the one called the Dream Man. It was his Karma to be born now and to carry on the work alongside his mother as she was the only clan member left alive besides him to carry on using the gift, or at times the curse, bestowed upon them. The gift of waking dreams and their ability to interpret those dreams. She taught him the ways of the Dream Clan; taught him to carry on the work of the clan, endowed with those special, precise gifts that were to be used to help humans who suffered or who had strayed from their Karma path. She knew she would soon die and at the appointed time, after she taught him all she knew, she did die.

Then the wolf pack descended from the mountains, but instead of devouring her and the Dream Man, they left her to the vultures as was the clan tradition for human remains to be devoured by vultures thus giving them life through the nourishment of their bodies. After all, what did it matter? For they knew their souls would be long departed and either still in the Void or being reincarnated once again.

The Alpha female wolf took care as did her pack to guide the boy to their mountain lair. There he would learn the ways of the wolves, and their insight into Nature which would be part of his life and his sense of life forever. Together with his knowledge from past lives and that passed on by his mother made him the most unique of all his clan and also the most powerful in collecting, interpreting dreams and using his unique skills and power to guide the humans to their Karma.

# STORIES OF THE COLLECTED DREAMS OF THE DREAM MAN

# THE LESSON OF THE FISH

> Very seldom do humans realize that other life forms also suffer at the hands of we humans. We think of them as beings, as things without feelings. One man learned this lesson and he learned it well, with the help of the Dream Man.

He loved to fish, loved to fish since his dad first took him fishing at age seven, more than sixty years ago. Now retired on a small lake, he loved to fish in the quiet of the morning, the solitude and peace of fishing alone on that small lake in a boat he made himself so many years ago. He called it his way of Zen Meditation, but the Dream Man called it a waking dream.

As he was thinking of what he may have done in his previous lives to deserve such a wonderful life, suddenly there was a jolt on the line that jarred him from his thoughts. Yes, he had hooked a fish, one of thousands he had caught over the decades, and he knew it was a nice one.

As he reeled in the fish and got it to the boat, with the help of the Dream Man, he was suddenly transported into the body of that fish. He became the fish with all the horror of being suddenly jabbed in the side of the mouth with a hook. He felt the sudden shock and quiver of his body as if struck by a thousand volts of electricity. He felt the pain, the total, heart-rendering, unbelievable feeling of being tortured, that he was going to die; die now as he was being pulled into the boat in sheer panic and unable to breath. He was suffocating to death.

He felt the pain of his total bodyweight being lifted by the hook, ripping apart his mouth, leaving a gaping hole and then yanked with brute force onto the bottom of the boat. He laid there floundering, trying to get back to that only life force he ever knew, the water. He tried so hard but his trying hastened his dying, slowed his trying as did his breathing and then suddenly, taking his last gasp, he died.

Immediately, the fisherman was slammed back into his own body. He sat there in his boat looking at the fish in total disbelief. He immediately knew what he must do. He grabbed the fish and placed it in the water, moving it back and forth so that the fish's gills and lungs could do the work of bringing oxygen back into the fish.

He then saw the gills of the fish moving in a normal rhythm and as he let go, the fish slowly swam away. At the same time, he felt a profound sense of gut-wrenching sadness for what he had done thousands of times before and what he had almost done again. He had never felt that way before in his entire life. No, not even when his wife had died. Nothing, nothing could match that strange, sudden sick-to-his-stomach feeling that overwhelmed him, bringing tears that would not stop flowing down his cheeks as he vomited the side of his boat.

He placed his fishing pole in the bottom of the boat, drove his boat to the shore, and walked away never to fish again, never to eat fish again.

As he has gotten older, he has thought of that day more than a decade ago this month. When he did, the tears again began to flow as he sits in his favorite chair at peace as never before, and overwhelmed with tears but this time, of happiness.

> The Dream Man smiled for being able to bring peace to one more sentient being.

# What Goes Around, Comes Around

> Sometimes, a person must suffer and get to the lowest level of existence before their true path of life can be found. On very rare occasions, it simultaneously happens to two people. This waking dream was just such an occasion that caused the Dream Man to get involved. Actually, he didn't know if this was really a dream or if he was receiving a prayer from her. He thought, that's all he needs, all these dreams and if he begins to hear other's prayers he will surely go crazy.

She started on him again, complaining about this and that, constantly, it seems almost 24/7, never letting up. She never stopped telling her son what a loser he was, why didn't he have a job? Telling him to get out and leave her in peace.

The old woman had reason to want him gone. Since she was crippled and in a wheelchair, she often needed help, but with his help came his yelling, his physical abuse as if it were all her fault he was a loser. In addition, there was his big mouth to feed at her expense.

*The Book of Waking Dreams*

The woman prayed each night for it to stop, for him to stop, for him to leave and yes, she confessed, she wished he would feel her pain and know what it was like for her to continue to live beyond her time.

She prayed and prayed often, not reserving prayers to the nighttime. She prayed, and prayed and prayed so much that her prayers consumed much of her day and night. Praying that he would know her life, either that or one of them would die and die now! Then she began having dreams and in those dreams, her prayers were answered. The dreams were so real, she felt the joy of them. She looked forward to sleeping and continued to have that recurring dream.

One day she awoke and her knees didn't hurt, the arthritis pains seemed to be gone. She tried walking, and to her great surprise, she could walk, walk slowly, but still she could walk without the support of a walker. She was so giddy, so joyful, she thought her heart would burst from the excitement.

Then suddenly she stopped, just stood there, realizing what may have happened. Had her prayers been answered? She got down on her knees and prayed, thanking God. Suddenly, she was jolted from her prayers by a cry for help, a god-awful scream coming from her son's bedroom. A wry smile crossed her face as she just froze there on bended knees. Then she knew, knew that her prayers surely had been answered. Her son now had her pain, had her ailments, and could not walk alone.

She slowly walked into his bedroom. She saw him there, unable to get out of bed on his own, unable to walk on his own, with his fingers curled, afflicted with arthritis as hers once were. He pleaded with her to help him. Help him get up and try to walk. She got him her wheelchair, which she always had handy when the walker was just not good enough, and helped him sit in it.

When he sat down, he suddenly turned and slapped her across the cheek, as he blamed her for his condition, but to his shock, it felt as if he had just hit himself. There was even a red mark of a hand, his hand, on his own cheek! She seemed to be unaffected. She just smiled and said, "If you want breakfast, wheel yourself into the kitchen."

Every now and then that day, he tried walking, bringing his fingers back to normal, even attacking her when she was close and not looking. Each time, it had the same affect. He just hurt himself. He even tried slapping himself to see if she would feel the pain in reverse. No, he just felt the pain of slapping himself.

Being his mother and yes, still deep down inside still a loving mother, she took care of him in the coming months. She helped him all she could. She never complained, always smiled and had a nice word to say to him. She fixed him his favorite dishes and little by little, they began to talk. She talked of her life, growing up, her mistakes in life and her joys.

He began to realize his mom was an extraordinary woman who had an extraordinary life. With each day they talked, he began to appreciate her more and more, and he told her so. He had once again grown to love and cherish her as the greatest mom ever.

He learned from her, from his mistakes too. His anger left him, he didn't recall when it happened but he knew why it happened. In those next few months, his mother taught him much about life, love, sacrificing for others, and the sheer joy that can come from just appreciating being alive, seeking all that life could offer and helping others.

One day, just as they were finishing one of their nightly talks, he confessed his love and appreciation for all that she had done for him, what she had taught him.

He hugged her as if he would never let her go. She whispered, "I love you so much son. I have prayed for this day." He felt her go limp in his arms and as he did so, his strength returned to him, but at a great price.

Now, this once angry young man, goes through his days, doing his best to help others, in every way possible to carry on the mission of his mother. The mission in his life, no matter what he did, he always tried to show compassion, love, charity and patience to all sentient beings.

> The Dream Man smiled as they both were sent on their planned Karma paths, with maybe a slight nudge from him to send him in the right direction and her into the Void.

# THE KEYS

> The Dream Man found that sometimes the worst of events are just providing the necessary yin (bad) to be able to get to the yang (good), and without it, the yang could not have been realized. Thus once again, showing the right path was the Middle Way, always in balance.

The bus dropped him off alongside the country road as it didn't go down his road – the road home. He had been gone a long time, at least it seemed. First the call-up of his unit, the chaos, the war in the desert. "How could they have ripped me from my home, my family?" he wondered at the time.

"It's bad enough," he thought, as he walked down that familiar dirt road, "trying to make a livin' as a poor farmer, but then to let my young wife and four young kids fend for themselves while I went off to help some others, some strangers, in a foreign land?"

He had signed up for the extra cash the Reserves offered him, not knowing they gave him that pay in peacetime so they could call on him in time of war. Well, he learned that lesson well enough now, but it was over. He was on his way home.

The call of the familiar doves woke him from his wondering mind. "That's all behind me now," he said quietly to himself. "I'm home now." He looked at the clear, blue sky; pure and clean, not like the big cities. He kinda smiled as he thought of those crazy city folk. "How could they live like that? I may be poor, but being poor in the country beat that crazy city livin' any day!" he said aloud then laughed.

It was the first time he laughed since he got the word about Amy's death and had the nightmares that followed. She was daddy's girl. He remembered their last day together. A big family dinner, everyone all dressed up. He could picture her yet in her pretty pink. It accented her rosy, red cheeks and blonde hair.

Walkin' along, he thought of the old key ring and the two keys on it. He had given one key to her the day he left, telling her that one key was the key to his heart and one key was the key to her heart. They both promised to keep each other's key safe until his return. Now, he was returning with mixed feelings of joy and sadness.

"I gotta be cheerful," he thought, wiping the tears from his eyes. As he looked up from the road, he saw her, at least he thought it was her. "No! It can't be," he thought, fearing the vision just down the road. "Amy! Amy! Is that you?" he cried, not believing and not wanting not to believe.

"It's me Daddy," she said softly. "I knew you would come. I just knew it. I got the key here. I've been takin' real good care of it Daddy. I really have." He stood there transfixed on his daughter's face. He took the key from her and gave her the one he had been keeping. He felt a peace come over him. "I gotta go now Daddy," she said. "It'll be alright. Don't cry Daddy and don't worry about me."

As she turned to go, he saw the almost transparent, silver-colored vapor rising from the grass and gliding along the ground. The vapor enveloped her and as it moved, seemed to be taking her with it, slowly gaining height as she moved towards the emerald-colored hills of summer.

Transfixed on his daughter, at first he didn't see the billowy vapor turning silver then white then taking on shapes, the shapes of angels' wings. As she neared the hills, he could see the angels, smiling as they took her hand, fading into the sky.

He walked on home, knowing that she was going to be fine; they all were going to be fine.

> Sometimes the Dream Man is able to smile and this was one of those times. He saw life in balance and proven once again that the Middle Way was the best way.

# HIS SIGNIFICANT, EMOTIONAL EVENT

> It is said that no matter the circumstances, once you had a significant, emotional event, it would change you to the core of who you were to who you were destined to be. This is the story of what Dream Man had collected and his influence on one such person.

He was a selfish person with an ego twice as large as his six foot, two inch frame. Dark and handsome according to the ladies and on the rise in the company. Some said he had it all, but he didn't think so. He wanted more, much more.

He thought he was invincible and nothing could stop him on his way to fortune and glory. Then the day came: he met another just like himself. A person who was vying for the same promotion, had the same goal in life – to have it all, adding even more stress to his already stressful life!

Then one day, it happened at the age of 47. A heart attack at work. It came suddenly, without warning. At first he thought, no way. It must be heart burn but his so-called heart burn got worse and worse, then he blacked out.

He recalled waking up in the hospital, seeing the face of a smiling nurse. "You are lucky to be alive," he vaguely heard her say and then he blacked out once again. A few days later, he awoke, weak, in shock and wondering how this could have happened to him.

More tests and doctor's consultations resulted in a doctor's order for some light exercise and a 30-day medically-driven vacation. He didn't want it but his boss forced him out of the office and he also found he was out of that promotion, at least for now. He went home to his condo and sat there trying to figure out what had happened and what to do for 30 days without going crazy.

He decided he might as well as get out of town and out of town he did. Not one to do things half-ass, he went out of town and all the way from New York City to Bangkok, Thailand, staying at a hotel overlooking the Chao Phraya River. For the first few days he walked a little, but pretty much hung around the hotel, swam a little, and generally watched the world go by from his suite overlooking the river.

The pace on the river was hectic and yet seemed to move at kind of a slow pace as boats and ferries moved up and down to their destinations with a rhythm all of their own. After a few days of that, he decided to see the sites of Bangkok and since so many of them were Buddhist Temples, he decided to tour a few. Grabbing a taxi, he headed to the oldest and reportedly, the largest, in Bangkok.

Why did he choose Thailand, a nation of Buddhists? He didn't know. But he seemed to be drawn to the country as he had been having dreams about Bangkok after his heart attack. Strange he thought, as he'd never been there and knew nothing about it so why dream of the place? The dreams were sort of blurry dreams, nothing very clear, more of thought of the place than visions of it. He arrived at the temple and decided to just walk around. As he walked around the grounds, he saw an old Buddhist monk sitting in the shade of an old Bodhi tree.

The monk smiled at him and beckoned him over. The monk asked him, "Why are you here?" He replied, "I just wanted to get away and decided on Bangkok and take a tour today." The monk had such a peace about him as if he was moving at a different pace, different from the world around him. He smiled in a way as if he knew something that others did not, something worth knowing, maybe the secret of life.

"No", said the monk with a smile. "Not why are you in Bangkok. Why are you in this world?" "I don't understand," he replied. The monk went on to explain that each human being is here to show love, to learn and to fulfill his or her Karma. "What have you learned? To whom have you shown love?" the monk asked him.

The man was hard-pressed to come up with a logical answer. Finally he said, "I don't know why I was born and what I am to accomplish in my life. All I know is that I have driven myself to grab as much out of life as I can." The monk corrected him, "You mean materialistic things out of life? What about those of a spiritual nature?"

He sat down and spent the day passing time with the monk, asking some questions, but mostly just listening. His questions led to more explanations and to more questions. And on it went. Throughout the next three weeks, they met daily under that tree and one day, just before he was ready to return home, he went to say good-bye to the monk.

When he arrived at the tree, the place where they had been meeting, the monk was not there. He asked a passing tour guide, whom he had seen leading tour groups around the temple, if she knew where the monk had gone.

She smiled and said, I didn't see any monk under the tree, but I have seen you sitting there and talking to yourself day after day. "Don't be alarmed," she said, "you're not crazy. Every once in awhile we tour guides see someone sitting under that tree talking to themselves. Some, like you, are from other parts of the world."

"You see", she went on, "there is a legend about an old monk who once died under that tree more than one hundred years ago and every now and then, someone sees him. I guess you needed his help. He always helps those in need. It is said that he knows the secret of life and helps people understand it and why they are here on this earth in this lifetime."

He went home, more confused than enlightened but also more at peace than ever before and knowing what he must do with the rest of his life, and he was determined to do it as much and as long as he could. He had a new priority in life. He was going to follow the old monk's advice to learn and to show love, compassion, patience and charity as much as possible.

From that day forward, he was at peace with himself, and eventually got that promotion. He donated the pay raise money to a charity as he had been doing with much of his money since his return.

Every year for more than ten years, he went back to Bangkok on the anniversary of his first visit. And every day for the following two weeks, he sat under that Bodhi tree and talked to that monk, learning more with each visit.

People walked by, laughing at the crazy American who came once a year and sat under the Bodhi Tree talking to himself. One day, people began to listen to what he was saying, the questions he was asking. They found that he did not seem crazy at all.

Soon, it was more and more difficult for him to return home. He found peace and enlightenment under that tree and people gradually began to gather near him to hear what he was saying, even though they did not know who he was talking to. He began to relay to those who sat down under that Bodhi tree what he had learned.

One day, the monk said he would come no more as his replacement had been found. He smiled and vanished. The American had found his Middle Way, his calling. Eighty-seven years later, he still sits under that tree talking of life, and its meaning to all who come by.

> The Dream Man for one of only a few times, was so happy to have been chosen to be the collector of dreams and setting events in motion. When he feels so mentally tired, frustrated and angry at his Karma, he often thinks of his efforts to send this man on his right Karma path, even though it took a great deal of effort to form into the vision of a Buddhist monk so often in order to do so. His efforts were able to positively influence so many others through this man.

## THE HUMMINGBIRD

> Once in a while, the Dream Man enjoys a waking dream as it brings him some happiness and hope for the future of we sentient beings. This was such a waking dream.

There was a lady who loved hummingbirds. In fact, she loved them so much that every season when it was about time for them to migrate through her area, she would hang many hummingbird feeders on the eves of her house. So many in fact, that hundreds of hummingbirds would show up to feed, that they fought for room and many even hung back on the nearby tree branches to wait their turn. There were so many that many didn't even have room to fight for space. She loved them so much, she constantly dreamt of them.

When the hummingbirds were around, that occupied her days, constantly busy refilling the feeders and buying more than ten pounds of sugar a week to feed these migrating little birds. One would think they could not drink and store that much of the sweet, red colored water, but they surely did.

She loved them so and often thought that when she died and could return to earth, nothing would please her more in her personal form

*The Book of Waking Dreams*

of Heaven than to return as a hummingbird for at least one migratory season so she could not only be part of the annual migration with hundreds, if not thousands, fellow hummingbirds, but also travel from one continent to another and view them from a different perspective.

A neighbor was not so inclined to put out feeders but he grudgingly had annually put out one token hummingbird feeder at her request. He reported that every year, after her death, one and only one hummingbird came by and drank from his feeder.

This hummingbird also stayed around longer and it seems only left when all the others had already migrated to the south. He often thought about his old neighbor and that hummingbird. He thought that if indeed there was a Heaven where wishes come true and there was life after death, she surely had returned as a hummingbird.

You probably know that feeling when every once in awhile, you have peace, contentment and all seems right with your world.

So, when the world seems to have it in for you and decided this was the day to beat on you and what can go wrong does, think of hummingbirds. It may bring a smile and life then doesn't seem too bad.

> The Dream Man liked to think of that pleasant waking dream and its results as it gave some hope about the future of we human beings and well, it just makes him smile and feel sort of warm and content inside to have had something to do with her return as a hummingbird.

## First Came the Children and the Birds Then Came Death

> On rare occasions, the Dream Man collects the dreams of someone gifted. Someone who knows Death, could sense it, and yes, in waking dreams, even predict Death, but also more than that, as if that gifted person was broadcasting her activities even when she was awake.
>
> Was she really awake or in a dream state? He couldn't figure that one out and after a while gave up trying and just accepted it for what it was, another collection from another sentient being. Yes, there are those that know when Death is near. Given that gift, but why? Maybe so they can help when Death is about to harvest its next victim? They know and yet, they stay silent as Death itself. Given the gift but never used, until it was her turn.

She worked the late shift at the assisted living home. They called it that because the residents had one foot in this world and the other in the world beyond death; they needed all the assistance they could get in one and help to prepare for the other.

Most of the time, the job was routine. Answer the intercom, dispense the meds, answer questions, but once in awhile the resident's intercom call complained of children making noises in the hallway. The resident said they would not shut-up no matter the threats. They even went out into the hallway to tell them to shut-up but they would not listen. The children would continue to play and to smile at the resident, as if waiting for something. That was always the "first early warning" call as she thought of it.

She would go into the hallway and found, as she suspected, no children, in fact no one. She would knock on the resident's door, who came out and said thanks for getting rid of the children. She would just smile and say your welcome as no sense in having any discussion on the topic. Why? She just figured the resident was more than halfway into dementia and besides, she knew why the children were there and didn't want to scare the resident by saying, "Oh they are here because you are soon to die."

After her shift was over, she would go to her car to go home and there he sat – a bird. A bird that seemed tame. So tame that it would not move from her path. That was early warning sign number two. Still, as the years went by, she kept silent, not using that gift at her command, the gift of knowing when someone would die. The early warnings gifts that could have been used to prepare Death's next victim and the victim's family, and of course the deaths continued as it does in life.

She rationalized not using the gift as not wanting to have her sanity questioned. After all, how long could she keep her job or get any job if she told people she knew when people were going to die?

Of course, the rationale included not wanting to get family members upset and sue her and the facility for "scaring the residents to death" – maybe sometimes literally. Furthermore, she hoped to avoid lawsuits where the lawyers twisted her gift and said she was not rational, not sane and she was threatening to murder the residents.

No, she thought it best to just keep quiet about it all, go about her business and let Death go about his. Time went on and one day she saw the children. She saw the bird too. Then she knew, it was soon to be her time. So, she prepared for his coming. She was ok with that and figured 117 years old was enough of life. One night he came for her. They found her the next morning, looking so peaceful and with just the slight hint of a smile on her face.

> The Dream Man was so saddened by this experience and that does not often happen. Usually, he has no such sadness but just goes about his business like some automation. However, this one affected him as he was powerless to influence her to use her gift.
>
> He felt so helpless as he knew she was given that special gift in order to provide compassion and love to those nearing death and to their families. He also was saddened because he knew she would return to the Void and from there her Karma for her next life would be set. He felt she would be regressed and would take so many more reincarnations to get back to where she was now.
>
> Such a waste, he thought. Such a waste. Made more so because this was the gift that she had asked for in the Void when preparing for reincarnation, but that story comes later.

# SHATTERED LIFE LIKE SHATTERED GLASS

> There are times when the Dream Man stays awake at night as some dreams are nightmares and one such dream places the Dream Man in the life of a broken man. Collecting and influencing dreams was one thing, but to take on that person, although rare, was never a pleasant experience for the Dream Man. However, sometimes such drastic measures are necessary. There is nothing more dangerous than a depressed, unemployed alcoholic with a gun. That was the case of Jimmy Lee Johnson.

He thought about his life – what a waste! He couldn't figure it out, but then again he never could. Why has so much gone so wrong so fast? Maybe because he started out different. Then again, he always thought of himself as different – not better than others, just different. He figured that is why he ended up where he is right now.

People thought that he was one to go his own way, not taking advice from anyone, even when it was sound advice as when it came to such things as staying in school. He always thought it was stupid to stay in school when he could get a job as a glass cutter. After all, he had always been good working with tools so why not use that skill? Besides, people made fun of him and said that he had strong hands but a weak mind. Well, maybe they were right but so what? He could work, pay his own way with nobody telling him what to do and how to live.

He had pretty much been on his own as far back as he can remember. Abandoned by his mother, never knowing his father and passed around from foster home to foster home, never staying long in one place. He was always considered a trouble maker even at a young age. That was fine with Jimmy Lee. He liked being considered "trouble".

That smugness changed to meanness after the economy went to hell and he lost his job. Not able to find work, he joined the unemployment roles, signed up for disability. Why not? Everyone else was doing it and his back got sore from time to time from leaning over that glass-cutting table those many years.

So, he and the boys met at the local bar, boosting each others' egos, blaming others for their fate and drinking their evenings away. Soon they were also drinking away their afternoons, then their mornings were added.

After a while, Jimmy Lee got tired of that too and tired of life. He started staying at home and drinking his three meals a day plus a drink for a snack and one for dessert.

He couldn't figure it out. Why had Life dealt him such a bad hand? He just couldn't admit that any of it was his fault. He walked around his place that the bank were foreclosing on. He looked at the windows and thought he probably cut that glass that made up the windows of the house. Well, if I did that work, then they belong to me and not the bank.

*The Book of Waking Dreams*

So, I can do with them what I please. He laughed, took his baseball bat and broke all the glass in all the windows and mirrors in the house.

After shattering all the glass, he took the last drops of what he considered the golden nectar of life, that alcoholic brew that came in a bottle, commonly called moonshine. Then he laughed and figured he will end up like all the glass that he shattered throughout his house. Then he put the end of the barrel in his mouth and pulled the trigger shattering his skull into hundreds of pieces where it scattered amongst the glass shards that lay around him.

> The Dream Man was also shattered in that he had involuntarily entered that man in order to save him, to show him the good that was possible for his Karma was known to the Dream Man and he saw that two paths were possible, and hoping he would choose the path of life.
>
> When Jimmy Lee died, a small part of the Dream Man died too and he once again cursed the Voice that forced him to collect dreams over and over and over and over again. The Dream Man knew that if Jimmy Lee had chosen life, he would have had such a positive influence on many others. Now, they too would not have his influence and the domino effect of suffering continued.
>
> The Dream Man knew that humans seldom looked at the influences they have over others – good and bad – and how that often causes more human suffering. Yes, he knew human suffering may never end, as they do not realize as they think in terms of this life and it being finite when they should think not of their human body but of their soul, which goes on for eternity and they should live their lives accordingly.

# THE PROMISE

> Sometimes, dreams are not really dreams but the mind recalling past lives and promises for the future. This is the story of one such "dream" that even enlightened the Dream Man on present life and life after life.

They met once again in that Void between death and reincarnation. They recalled their past lives together, as souls in the Void are able to do. These two had a strong connection over many lifetimes. They had gone through many lives together in different roles.

They had learned that their reincarnations were usually based on their desires, as long as their roles led them to learn and love more than they had in the previous lives; thus, always improving with each reincarnation on their way to Nirvana.

Once again, they discussed what their relationship should be in their next lives. This time, she wanted to return again as a female and have the gifts of compassion that would help those sentient beings by allowing her to see in advance or in real-time those who are in pain, suffering, in sorrow, ill, or ready to die. With that insight, she then wanted to find ways to help them through whatever compassionate means she could.

She felt such a gift would help her learn what she had known little of in past lives: the lives of others who suffer and how to help them. In her past lives, her focus was mostly on her own need for self-centered learning and loving herself – not in a selfish way but she had learned that if you do not love and respect yourself as a sentient being, you could not show true compassionate and love to others.

He on the other hand decided to stay in the Void as he was unsure as to what his next role should be in his reincarnated life, e.g. how to increase his experiences and knowledge, learning more of everything in life and showing more love to all sentient beings. He knew that in showing love, one must incorporate into that word, compassion and also a respect for all individual sentient beings as unique, precious spirits.

So, she was reincarnated and endowed with the great gifts as she had asked. As she grew older, her ability to see illnesses, sadness, sorrow in people sometimes before it even occurred and of course in real-time, matured as she matured. She also began to see signs as to when people would die – not the exact date but pretty much within 24–48 hours of seeing signs through them and about them.

The problem with reincarnation is that new lives, although leaving a history in one's mind of past lives, most don't know it, except for those who spend decades meditating without the noise of the world blocking such knowledge. Things like getting an education, working, getting married, having kids, paying bills, and the general stresses of everyday life gets in the way. Thus, it is often difficult to know what path to take in life. Although we often have a sense of it, due to the noise in our lives, we "feel" it but often do little to take that pre-destined path.

By ignoring that "feeling", that "inner voice", we must then regress in our reincarnations until we do take that path. If not, we cannot move on to the next plane of existence that we must all eventually move to.

So, as her maturity grew, so did her gifts. She gravitated towards a career as a nurse, without her knowing why but just a feeling as something she should do. She did not know that it was in keeping with her reincarnated desire to show more compassion and help others in need – to once again learn and to show love.

At the time, she also did not realize that the great increase in her abilities, her senses to see sentient beings in pain, sorrow, and even ready for death, was needed for her to accomplish what she wanted to accomplish in this life. Her life's noises had gotten in the way. Therefore, she treated these great gifts as curses.

Her lives' partner sensed all this while in the Void and decided that he must return to help her. He must return so that he could remind her that what she had was a great gift: to be able to sense the pain and pending death of others, and then use her gifts to help relieve their pain with compassion or help prepare them for death and reincarnation.

He returned to help her, to remind her that her curse was in fact a great gift. Thus, he sacrificed his own needs for learning what he needed to learn to help her.

Ironically, as it happens when Karma intervenes as the great guide in our lives, in helping her, he in fact was also learning more about the meaning of life for all sentient beings. By helping her, he was also showing compassion, patience, charity and love to her and all the sentient beings he encountered.

He knew when he had helped her, got her to see her great gifts, and on that path she was destined to take in this life, he would die. That was fine with him. He would wait for her in the Void once again where they could talk about their next lives together.

> The Dream Man was pleased with having helped make this happen for both of them. He knew their next reincarnations would bring them to a higher level of humanity and on their way to Nirvana, if they so chose that part of the Void when given the opportunity.

# HAPPY BIRTHDAY FROM MOM

> Sometimes dreams occur to humans that take on a life all of their own. Especially for humans who have special gifts that they may or may not know they have, or have a fear of them and push them as far back in the recesses of their mind as they can.
>
> One such woman knew she was gifted but did not know how gifted. However, she was about to learn about one such gift. The Dream Man not only collected her dreams of her mom, but was about to influence them and her new experience of her mom.

Marie realized she had special gifts since she was about five years old. She not only saw and talked to dead people but over time learned to convey their messages back to their loved ones. She did so quietly, so as not to draw attention from news media, others who would try to exploit her or tear her down as a fraud because they envied or feared her.

Some feared her when they found out she could tell if they would be cursed by cancer, dementia or other diseases. She even saw the signs telling her when someone was about to die. So, those that knew her great gifts, shunned her and would rather bury their heads in the sand than know the truth about themselves.

Marie often dreamt of and thought of her mother, dead some years back. She knew very little of her, as her mom had died when she was very young. Even though Marie was often able to talk to dead people, her mother never came to her even though Marie sought her out in her mind on many occasions.

Marie was reaching her 60th birthday soon. Her life was not what one would call a very happy one overall. Yes, there were moments of happiness here and there, but in general, she thought her life pretty much was lived under a black cloud. When things seemed to start to go good for her, something happened that knocked her back down. She was one who some would call a person that couldn't buy a break.

During one stretch of being totally beaten down by life, she wished, hoped, prayed so much that her mother would find her, bring her some comfort, for Marie was hurting more than ever as she approached her half century of struggling on this earth.

On the eve of her birthday, alone, feeling old, tired and drained both mentally and physically, she fell into a restless sleep, even crying in her sleep. It was then that Marie saw her come into the room. She saw her through her reflection in a mirror. Her mom was dressed in jeans, blue blouse and white coat. She was holding a beautiful two layer, white-frosted cake with a circle of candles around the edges. Her mom smiled and said, "Happy Birthday child." Marie was fixated and did not know what to say. Her only emotion was the tears streaming down her cheeks.

Her mom said, "Child, I am here for you always. I have always watched you but I was powerless to help you. I am still powerless to help you, but you are not powerless to help yourself." Marie said, "I can't Mom. I tried. I tried and failed so many times over the years. Please help me Mom."

Her mom said, "Child, I am so sorry, but you were given such special gifts and you are such a special and wonderful woman. You must use your gifts to help find your way in life. You are destined to find happiness in this life my dear. You just have to trust your heart more and your mind less. Your power comes from your heart and your logic from your mind. Time to start trusting your heart."

Marie was able to see her mom from time to time but mostly they just smiled at each other, comforting Marie as she was able to sleep a little better knowing her mom was watching over her, loved her and was there for her.

To this day, Marie continues to waiver between her mind that she trusts and her heart and soul that she does not want to trust. She continues to search her way through her life not knowing that the Karma path was clear if she would only see with her heart and soul and not with her mind.

*The Book of Waking Dreams*

The Dream Man watched Marie from time to time. He was saddened because all he saw was her focusing solely on work and immediate family. That was her life. He saw her aging prematurely, being physically and mentally beaten down by life not knowing that happiness was in reach if only she would look beyond her physical environment and look into her everlasting soul that would lead to her Karma and on to the right path in this life and the lives yet to come.

Ironically, she was trying so hard to focus on family, worried about family but didn't realize that her current life was slowly killing her and didn't consider what would happen to her family when she was gone. Like others, she always thought she had more time.

He knew of her great gifts, the kindness in her heart and even the wanting and hoping of her very soul that she did not know. He shook his head each time as to her plight. He could see the path she should take and had not taken. He could not interfere in her Karma. Only she could find the way but only if she trusted her heart, believe what her heart, her soul, was trying to tell her.

He wondered, "Will she ever find true happiness?" Even he did not know the answer to that question. So from time to time he would be there as she slept and watched her and her mom. Seeing no change, he sadly time after time walked away hoping that some day, some way, she would follow her heart, find her Karma's path and live the joyous life he knew she was destined to live – if only – but then again, he had been wrong before.

# THE SPIDERS

> On occasion, the Dream Man collects some dreams where animals and insects are involved. It is rare but he has had that experience on occasion. Animals and insects play a vital role in the dreams and lives of many humans. One such story is about thousands, hundreds of thousands that surround a woman's bedroom as she slept. She feared them and feared each night they appeared in her waking nightmares.

Susan was a single mom raising kids over the decades, working, fighting to survive in a world that seemed to always place the odds of getting ahead against her. Like many, Susan feared many types of insects, and one of those most feared were spiders, any kind of spider. So, it figures how Karma weaves its web so-to-speak that when she least wanted to see them, least expected to see them, they came in her waking nightmares not by the hundreds, not even by the thousands, but by the hundreds of thousands.

They did not come every night, no, that would be too easy, too easy to become accustomed to seeing them. No, these black spiders, almost flat, two-dimensional spiders came when she least expected them. They came through the walls, from under the bed, from light fixtures, from wall plugs, for under the bedroom door, from the closet. If there was a way for spiders to get into her room, they did.

She hated them, feared them with their hairy bodies and legs, beady eyes, and weird, ugly mouths. She thought of them as the devil's helpers, his minions there to put fear in her for no other reason as it gave the "evil one" pleasure to unleash them upon her.

One night she had enough. She decided not only to not fear them but to communicate with them. After all, in dreams many things are possible. So, in her nightmare, she yelled at them to stop! Stop right now and to her surprise, they did. However, she found little comfort in that as they all suddenly turned to look at her, all those eyes focused on her. They stared at her as if waiting for her to speak. Finally she asked, "Why are you doing this to me? Why are you here scaring the hell out of me?"

Finally, one spider spoke to her mind and said, "We are here for you Susan. We are here to protect you. Do you not know you cause us to be summoned due to your fears, your worries? You cause us to come, ordered by another when you are in fear and you are in fear of many things." Susan said, "That is not true! I don't have any fears except of creatures like you!". The spider said, "Think about it Susan. You don't worry about your job, your family, making ends meet, your lovely daughter, you finding happiness in this lifetime, especially as you get older, children grow up and leave? Are you saying you do not worry about such things? You don't fear growing old alone?". Susan said, "No, well, of course I have concerns, everyone does of such things. All humans deal with that in life."

The spider said, "Susan, you need us. We are summoned by the Dream Man who knows your fears. He sees them, feels them when he is with you in your dreams and even in your nightmares. We are his messengers, his minions sent to protect you from your fears but you don't seem to understand that. We are many as your fears are many and they are strong."

"You need not fear us Susan. Isn't it bad enough that you fear your future whether that be tomorrow or many years from now? You worry so. You find no peace within yourself so how do you expect to find it anywhere if not in yourself?"

Susan listened as he "spoke" of her life, the potentials she could experience but does not out of fear of "what if this, what if that, this is messy, this is not perfect, something may go wrong" and all the worries that envelope her sleep and even her waking times.

Over the next few nights, the spiders returned every night as they talked to her. Gradually, the number of spiders coming in the night decreased as her fears, her nighttime worries decreased. Sometimes there were more than other nights.

> The Dream Man had sent his minions to her, he longed for the time that they would not have to be sent to her at all. He longed for the time when she could sleep all night, peacefully and deeply having found the true meaning of her life. He longed for that time as much as she did. He still waits and still sends the protective spiders to her bedroom, some nights more, some nights less.

# THE LITTLE GIRL WHO DEFEATED "THE EVIL ONE"

> She was a product of her African upbringing and as such feared the evil spirit everyone just called "The Evil One". She couldn't remember when she did not have nightmares of this evil spirit that could change into many forms. The Dream Man on these rare occasions when he collected her dreams, felt sorry for this young girl and decided to help her.

Samantha, to her friends, Sam, was one whose mind excelled on many levels, especially for one only six years old, with the ability to see visions of the dead and spirits, both good and evil. Her mind was also restless and often troubled by the nightmares brought on by stories told by Zulu shamans of this evil spirit that can cause so much mischief and harm to humans, especially harmful to school-age children such as Sam.

No matter the evening weather, when Sam had her nightmares of "The Evil One", as he was called, which happened quite often in her young life, she would wake up often screaming and always in a cold sweat, shaking from fear.

Her parents could not help her, her friends could not help her, doctors, even psychiatrists and psychologists could not help her. She felt she was cursed and beyond all help. Surely, one day soon she would either die of fright or the The Evil One would in fact eat her in her nightmare and she felt in real life she would surely die from that nightmare.

The next morning, Sam told her parents of her dream and they decided to do as she had asked. In addition, they placed a brick under each bed leg as part of her nightmare-dream; she saw herself lying in bed and she thought it strange that her bed had a brick under each bed leg.

The next night she started to have that nightmare again but suddenly dreamt of being awake and seeing the The Evil One for the first time as it was all red. It was an ugly, evil looking spirit but she was no longer afraid. It tried to climb into her bed but could not, no matter how it tried, as the bed was too high for this small creature. She felt safe and she smiled at it. The Evil One could not bear that as it thrived on fear and Sam no longer showed or felt any fear. Angered but powerless, he left and Sam never had a nightmare of it again.

The Dream Man was powerless to help her by ridding her of this evil spirit. However, he could plant a dream in her head the next time the nightmare occurred as that was the only time when her link to the spirit world was open. The next night he collected her nightmare as it was happening and placed a dream in it, and thus her mind, of adding a red coloring to all the water bowls in and around the house for he knew that The Evil One is invisible when he drinks water, which it always did before entering the homes and dreams of humans. However, when the water is red, it becomes visible and once visible to humans, it loses its power of fear. At times, in her sleep, when it tried to again penetrate her mind, the Dream Man sent Sam the vision of her in bed and the feeling of being safe. Each time, the Evil One left until the time many months later when it never returned.

# Young Heart, Old Soul

> This waking dreamer is one of the few very young ones that the Dream Man has encountered in recent years. He doesn't know why but he seldom receives dreams, or nightmares, of the very young. He suspected that it was because being so young and just started on their Karma path that there was nothing for him to do to guide, or otherwise impact their lives as he could with adults. Besides, when so young, they were more in a "pure" state.

She was so very young at five years old, but the Dream Man thought that she seemed to be so mature for such a young person. She also seemed to be an old soul in the body of a child. He knew that on rare occasions this sometimes happened and it always happened for a reason.

The Dream Man's experiences taught him that such children had very specific reasons for being born and set on a special Karma path. Joy, as she was called, was no exception. She had special powers such as seeing the dead, various good and bad spirits, having visions and premonitions. Furthermore, she had the power to influence the dreams of others.

*The Book of Waking Dreams*

The Dream Man sensed this and had hoped that she may be his replacement since he was so bone-dead tired after over 200 years of life and most of it as the Dream Man having to absorb, interpret and influence the dreams, and nightmares, the lives, of so many over the centuries.

Joy was always a special child and as such, she knew that her life must begin in the Yin cycle before moving into the Yang cycle. She knew this because she remembered being in the Void where her life, her Karma, was set. She saw her birth mother and knew in advance she would have to suffer so she would know the difference between Yin and Yang. She needed that to fulfill her Karma of relieving the suffering of other sentient beings.

She also saw her future adoptive mother: a kind, loving, spiritual soul also with special gifts, mostly different but with some similarities to hers. She knew she was there to suffer, then join her adoptive mother who was also suffering. She knew she was there to be her adoptive mother's spiritual guide as well bring her joy and lead her to her right Karma path.

When Joy was born into the world of pain and suffering caused by her birth mother, she knew, even when she laid in her crib, what was to come. Less than a year old, she could talk but stayed silent. She spent her quiet time in deep meditation and in the waking dream state seeing visions of things to come; as well as seeing ghosts and spirits. Some there were her guardians, while others represented evil. Since she was so pure of heart and soul, these malevolent spirits tried to destroy her. She was plagued with visions of vicious insects, and malevolent spirits. She also saw others that seemed to be good, but she was still young, inexperienced and didn't know for sure.

At the appointed time, she was given to her adoptive mother, Marie, and her transition from Yin to Yang began. However, it was not to be an easy journey and in her waking dreams she continued to be attacked, and even when she was in a waking state, she was being attacked. The malevolent spirits were becoming more and more desperate. They also started to attack Marie in hopes of destroying her relationship with Joy. After all, they saw the special gifts of Marie that could be used to help protect Joy if she ever learned how to use such gifts.

The guardian spirits countered with protective ghosts, spirits and insects. Sometimes, Joy and Marie both saw thousands of spiders in their waking dreams. These were their protectors and messengers sent to them by Joy's protectors to counter the works of the malevolent spirits.

Although an "old" soul, Joy was also a child and often she saw ghosts and insect spirits that frightened her, especially as they came all of a sudden at what seemed to be haphazard times. For example, when sitting in the car driven my Marie, the black shadow of a man would suddenly appear next to their moving car. Joy could not discern his demeanor nor the details of him. Was he a protector or there to capture her soul, destroy her Karma's path? In an instant he was gone, back again and gone. Joy feared something bad would happen if Marie ran him over, but she never did.

The malevolent spirits continuously tried new and old tactics as they could see that as Joy aged, her power to defeat them, to fulfill her destiny continued to get stronger. They had to act now and they constantly used various methods to attack her, frighten her in her waking dreams; however, so far nothing seemed to be working.

*The Book of Waking Dreams*

Joy always knew that one of the primary reasons why she was born was that as she matured in her powers as well as her physical being, was to bring joy to others, beginning with Marie. Marie would be her "test case". Thus, while in the Void, she chose the name "Joy" and caused her birth mother to name her thus. Joy knew that her Karma road would not be easy. It was not suppose to be easy as only through pain and suffering could she ever understand the misery, pain and suffering of others and be able to be empathetic, show them love, patience, compassion, charity and help relieve their suffering.

Marie also had a difficult life full of pain, suffering with little happiness. When it seemed happiness was within reach, the malevolent spirits made sure to turn her Yang into Yin for they knew the powers she had before she did. Powers that once harnessed, could also be used for good. By enhancing her gifts, her power to use compassion, love, charity and patience, Marie would have strong power to help end human sufferings and thus weaken the powers of the malevolent spirits, who could only thrive on human misery and suffering.

Joy knew that Marie suffered both physically due to abuse and illnesses. So Marie put up barriers against any possible joy that may come with the right person, her soulmate. Marie thus focused and only trusted her immediate family. That was her life. No life existed but through them. Joy knew that had to change.

Joy knew her main purpose in this life was to bring joy to sentient beings, help relieve their suffering. One of her powers was the ability to influence the waking dreams of others. The Dream Man was so happy to watch Joy's development as he knew she indeed would be his future replacement. So he watched with great interest in her development and did not try to influence her waking dreams or her life in any way, as to do so may lead her to the wrong path and away from him, from replacing him.

Joy began by identifying Marie's soulmate as Marie evidently didn't remember him nor her pact with him in the Void to meet once again and be together once again, to love each other once again. Also, they were to join together to bring compassion, love, charity, and patience to as many suffering, sentient beings as would be possible in their remaining life together before they returned to the Void to plan their next adventure.

Joy brought the two together and once they met, Joy knew that they would feel a connection between them. She knew that would not be good enough as one can lead a horse to water…. Joy caused Matthew to have waking dreams of Marie and also of Joy. At first, Matthew was skeptical and thought such waking dreams were more of hopes and wishes with no chance of ever coming true so he constantly put them in the back of his mind.

Joy found that this would not be as easy as she had thought. She caused him to have waking dreams of her needing help from him and the best way was to cause Marie to be in need of assistance. At first, it only partially worked as he did not make the connection she wanted. So in the third waking dream, she inserted herself more forcefully and as Matthew completed his assistance to Marie and was leaving, Joy cried out, "Daddy, don't leave!". Matthew was shocked by that dream and didn't know what to make of it.

Then came the day when a festival brought the three of them together in what seemed to be a coincidence, but in fact was part of Joy's elaborate plan: Joy and Matthew met. When she saw Matthew, she ran to him all smiles and hugged him. Matthew was shocked as he had not known Joy before that meeting. Throughout that evening, Joy spent time with him and won him over. He asked Marie about Joy and learned of her life. He felt this kinship with her. What a strange development he thought. He always felt Marie was his soulmate from the first day they met. However, now there was Joy. He wondered how and why she seemed to be so familiar to him too.

While she was influencing Matthew, she later caused Marie to have a waking dream of Matthew being with Marie. Joy had hoped that this would bring them together – as together they were meant to be. However, the malevolent spirits were not going to make that easy. They had their own plans to negate Joy's efforts. After all, happiness only came to these spirits when others were in misery, suffering.

The malevolent ones had more influence and control over humans whom they had made miserable. They knew that human beings who were of small minds and small hearts wanted others to be as miserable as they were jealous of those who were happy. So, some conspired, making false accusations against both Marie and Matthew. With much difficulty, these conspirators were defeated but in doing so, the malevolent spirits also could claim victory for they caused Marie and Matthew to maintain more of an arms-length distance to avoid future allegations of any wrongdoing. Marie also kept Joy from physically spending time with Matthew.

Joy knew that but still used her waking dreams powers to keep both her and Marie in Matthew's dreams and waking thoughts. Joy also tried to use her influence with Marie, but Marie also having powers, and especially physical control over Joy's life, she made it difficult for the three of them to be together.

The Dream Man was saddened over these recent events as it seemed that things were progressing nicely along the right Karma paths where their three paths would intersect and integrate into one path where together, they would show compassion, patience, love and charity and together form a formidable force to defeat the malevolent spirits and ease the misery, pain and suffering of sentient beings.

The Dream Man also feared that if Joy could not accomplish the task of reuniting the three of them, she would not be able to eventually take his place. In looking back, he wished he had interfered to assist Joy. However, it was too late for that now.

The Dream Man would continue to wish, hope and watch while Joy continued to try to influence these two lost soulmates and reunite them as they were meant to be. Joy believed she could make it happen, eventually, but "eventually" was not what Joy had naively thought. She thought it would happen immediately.

This experience also taught her a valuable lesson and that lesson was that humans as spiritual beings were not aways predictable as they lost their way and strayed from their Karma's path. It also taught her that the malevolent spirits were strong, and she not as strong as she once thought.

So, Joy continues to send both waking dreams to both Marie and Matthew; continues to send waking dreams and thoughts of her to Matthew; tries to influence them to join their Karma paths; tries to provide Matthew opportunities to meet her so that her influence can be its strongest by combining her physical presence with her spiritual presence.

It is said that "hope springs eternal" and both Joy and the Dream Man are hopeful; and thanks to Joy's influence, the hopes of Matthew continue.

# Books Don't Bring Enlightenment

> Dreams often bring truth and lead the way to the path to Enlightenment. This is one such dream that was captured by the Dream Man.

She loved books, they were her lover, her family, her companion. She believed that all she needed was books. She needed them more than anything else in life. She thought that her books would lead her to the meaning of life and Enlightenment. She craved for isolation and worked to have the money it takes to live such a life.

Her goal was finally reached and she moved to an island and into a cabin, away even from the others that moved there for isolation. She spent every waking moment reading, studying, learning everything she could find that she hoped would eventually lead her to discover the "meaning of life" and thus to Enlightenment.

Day and night she read until her eyes burned red and blurred until she could no longer read a word. Then she collapsed into a deep sleep and, once awake, she once more continued reading, devouring every word, every page, every book she could find that even remotely related to the meaning of life and Enlightenment.

Even in sleep, she tried to dream what she had read, tried to learn even in a waking dream state. This went on for years and years as she grew into an old woman. She was a brilliant scholar by then. She committed so much to memory and if she could not remember, she knew which book held the answer.

She wrote brilliant theses on all sorts of topics discussing the meaning of life, the philosophy of life and, yet, her quest for the true meaning of life and Enlightenment continued to allude her. She decided that books were not enough; she must travel the world to experience life and maybe in doing so, find its meaning and Enlightenment. She gave up her isolated life and traveled the world seeking answers to the meaning of life, to find the path to Enlightenment.

Finally, one day, she met an old man in a temple ruins in an isolated area of Tibet, who smiled at her as she walked by. She smiled and continued her exploration of the ruins. Then she moved on. At another temple she saw what seemed to be the same old man again who once again smiled at her. This happened again and again as she visited old Buddhist ruins, old temples, new temples. Anywhere there were Buddhist people praying, in meditation, he was there.

Finally, she sat down with the monk and asked why he was everywhere she went. He answered her with a question. He asked her why she was visiting all those places. She replied that she was trying to learn, to find the meaning of life and the path to Enlightenment. She told him her story, about the thousands of books she had read and studied. She told him the sacrifices she had made as she wanted to find the path to Enlightenment, to find the meaning of life.

He just listened, smiled as if knowing something special, something that she had not been able to grasp. When she had told her story, she figured why not ask him about Enlightenment as a sort of afterthought.

So, she asked this old man, "Do you know the meaning of life and the path to Enlightenment?" and to her surprise he said that yes he did indeed know that which she sought. He told her the path is through the Tao. He said that she could not find wisdom except through the Tao and through the Tao she will find Enlightenment.

She said that she had read all there was to read on such things but what she had learned did not help. He replied, "Of course not! Reading may give you knowledge but knowledge will not give you wisdom. If you try to define or describe the Tao, you are on the wrong path. It cannot be described. It is not some physical object, it is not some feeling." He then went on to explain that even people who cannot read or write have found Enlightenment. "Now you are probably wondering how they did it," he said with a smile. He told her that it is because they sought Enlightenment within themselves. She looked at him somewhat perplexed.

The old man smiled once again and shook his head and explained that in each of us resides the Tao and Enlightenment. You cannot find it by seeking it from external sources. Seek it within you. It is there waiting for you.

"Is the same true for the meaning of life?" she asked him. "There is no meaning of life as you think of it, but so you can understand it a little, know this: Life consists of a path and on that path, your path, no matter how many dead-ends, twists and turns, valleys and mountains that your path takes you, the path will lead you eventually to wisdom through the Tao to Enlightenment. Many people have taken hundreds, even thousands of lifetimes to discover that simple truth."

"I don't know how to do that," she sobbed, "I am so tired. I have worked so hard and now you tell me it has been all for nothing!" The old man said "It has not been for nothing, it has brought you to this place and this time."

Now she understood. Now she knew how to find that path and was ready to begin her path to Enlightenment as she said, "Master," (using that term for the first time) "may I follow you on your journeys?" He said, "Of course, that is why I have been waiting for you all these years."

> The Dream Man was thankful that there are those sentient beings who can be influenced to help others in his place. The wise man was once such person.

# BETTER LATE THAN NEVER

> The Dream Man thought this set of dreams were unusual. Two people who had met, destined to be together but didn't realize it until he gave them the nudge.

Rebecca, known to her friends as Becky, first met Martin about 15 years ago at a conference. Since then she couldn't get him out of her mind. She thought of him in waking dreams and in deep dreams, some even bordering on pornographic dreams. At first the dreams were few and far apart but as time went on they increased. Then when he began writing a monthly article for a journal her publisher assigned her to edit, they corresponded by emails.

Her feelings for him were there from the first time they met but she said nothing since he didn't seem to show any special feelings for her at the time. So, small talk about conference topics and then they said goodbye. She kept thinking of him from the beginning but now, those feelings and her dreams of him began to intensify and happen more often.

They kept in touch via email a few times a year talking about books, writing, how life was treating them, this and that.

*The Book of Waking Dreams*

Martin had almost the identical experience. He couldn't stop thinking of her but kept at arms length as he thought she was nice but did not care for him other than a kind of friend. Over time, his waking dreams, his deep dreams began taking on a more sexual aspects. He dreamt of her lips, how it would be to kiss her, hold her close to him and more.

He decided to take his time as was not sure of her feelings. He increased his emails to her and she responded in kind. Soon they were emailing daily while their dreams began to become increasingly almost the same. They began to sense each others moods too.

> The Dream Man smiled as he continued to influence their dreams to nudge them closer and closer together. However, he was also losing patience with both of them as they should see by now they were meant to be together. After all, it had been almost 15 years!
>
> Finally, he had them both dream of meeting and sharing a few weeks together to help them on their way down their Karmic path. They met, hugged, and it was then that both felt an overpowering feeling of love and even familiarity.
>
> The Dream Man smiled as he knew they would soon be spending the rest of their lives together in love; a pure deep love. Neither would ever be alone again. Their past broken hearts would slowly heal each others. Their love would shield them from the hurt of the world.
>
> Although they did not know it, they had been together in past lives and they will be together in future lives. The Dream Man hoped that in their future lives it would not take so long for them to find each other and once that had happened, they would quickly realize their destiny together.

## **BEAR THE GUARDIAN**

> Sometimes a person needs more than another human when lonely or in need of comfort. Such was the case with Jack. In this case, the Dream Man sent him a waking dream because Jack's anger blocked his vision of why his beloved Bear had died, and yet was not dead.

Jack had come home from work and had found his beloved, young German Shepherd dog, Bear, dead. He had gotten Bear from a German Shepherd rescue shelter when he was only one year old. Jack lived alone, was often considered introverted, a loner – and he was – as he had no confidence in what he saw was the worst of humanity. So, he avoided humans as much as possible, and so he decided to get a dog. Not just any dog, but a dog known for its strength, intelligence, size and being fiercely loyal. Jack wanted almost what he would consider an equal, one that he could even play rough and wrestle with.

Bear was a big 117 pound, black and tan male and Jack was told at the shelter that he was unpredictable and considered dangerous. He was being considered to be put to sleep as "un-adoptable". Jack looked into Bear's eyes and they seemed to bond immediately. They both knew at once, they were kindred spirits and meant for each other.

*The Book of Waking Dreams*

So, Jack took Bear home and, for three years, they were the greatest companions, even friends. They knew each other so very well and could even sense their moods. Through Bear, Jack became more sociable as people commented on him as they took their walks and played in the dog park.

When Bear suddenly died of an enlarged heart, Jack withdrew back into his shell and even more so. He was so very angry at the world, at everything, at everyone. He hid within himself and hated life.

Then one night, Jack had a waking dream. He was not awake, and yet not asleep. He was sitting in the living room in a small house where he could see both the screen doors of the open doors in the front and back of the house. He saw what looked to be two massive, Rottweilers angrily growling by the front door. He quickly ran and closed the door for fear they would break through the screen door and attack him, although they were facing away from him. He didn't want to take the chance and didn't want to look at them for fear they would turn on him.

He then saw two large dogs, whose breed he thought to be mastiff. They were huge, all black. They were lying down, quietly by the back screen door, with the solid wood door, like the front door, wide open, but these two also did not look friendly but they didn't make a sound as they stared at him.

He was frozen in his chair as the back door was too far and he feared that if he got up and went towards them to close the door, they would break through the screen and attack him. No doubt they too looked fierce. Then he saw him appear between them and sat down, looking, staring into his eyes. It was Bear. Jack couldn't believe it. It was so real, as if he was alive. They looked into each other's eyes and then Jack realized why he was there.

Jack just knew and that knowing brushed away his anger, his bitterness and brought him a calmness he had not known since Bear's death so many months ago. Bear was there and brought his companions to be with Jack as his guardians and so he would never be alone again.

Bear brought peace to Jack, calmed him and soon brought a smile that Jack had not shown in so long. Now Jack knows that wherever he goes, he is not alone, Bear and his companions are there with him. His truest friends and Guardians.

> The results of the waking dream also brought a smile to the face of the Dream Man as he seldom has such opportunities to send original dreams to someone. However, since the Dream Man also knows about other life forms, he had sensed Bear was as confused and lost as Jack. To see them together, well, it was one of the few times he was happy to be the Dream Man.

# HELP ME! I WANT TO FALL

> The Dream Man never ran into a case such as that of Jack Kingman. Usually, if he could not influence an outcome, told to just observe but not interfere, he always somehow knew that for whatever reason, things always seemed to turn out ok, until now.

Jack had been one of those who had seen more of his share of misery in his past middle age life. It was during his tumultuous youth, his days of military service in Southeast Asia, and afterwards where he seemed to always be the one walking under that black cloud.

Just when things were looking good for him, something happened to destroy his hopes, his dreams. He had gone through several marriages where he seemed to have finally found the one that he thought would be his salvation only to turn out to be Life just teasing him and then ripping out the Yang from his life and Yin slamming him back to his dark hole that he seemed to never be able to crawl out of.

To add to Jack's misery over the decades, he had constant dreams, or maybe someone would call them nightmares, of falling off of various high places, whether they be bridges, cliffs, or evening looking down from his window seat on commercial airliners.

He always had been one that had a fear of heights. No, not a fear of heights like normal people had. No, Life would not be so ordinary for Jack. You see, Jack didn't fear heights because he was afraid of falling, he feared heights because he always wanted to fall, to jump. He wanted to fall with eyes closed, legs stretched out, arms stretched out like wings, feeling the wind in his face, buffeting his body. He imagined the sheer joy of such freedom. His dreams always encompassed that feeling, that wanting to jump, to fall free.

Jack always awoke just before he sensed he would soon hit the ground. Some believe that if you dream of falling and have your eyes open seeing yourself rapidly coming upon the ground, when you hit the ground you would literally die in your sleep. Jack never worried about that, actually, never thought of that. Maybe that saved him, who knows? No, Jack just wanted to fall and yes, he wanted to die.

His dream of his falling death increased as his latest chance of happiness rapidly deteriorated. He thought he had met "The One", the woman that he so loved and he thought loved him just as much in return. They had known each other for some time and over time, gradually both admitting that they were meant for each other; however, there was a slight catch. She was married, albeit unhappy in a separated relationship, but married nonetheless.

They talked of their love, planned to be together, in fact were on occasion, but he finally realized that Life would not allow him that happily ever after joy in his life. There seemed no end to their limbo status. When Jack had realized that once again, happiness was beyond his reach, his dreams of jumping, of soaring and the sheer joy of it increased exponentially. Then one day, Jack decided to make his dreams come true. He went to that cliff and soared.

The Book of Waking Dreams

> The Dream Man was in total shock, disbelief. Never before had something like this happened in his over 300 years of life. How could the Voice, Karma, allow such a tragedy to occur? The Dream Man realized, he was losing his power to influence dreams. Then he knew, his time would soon come to an end. That brought him some peace and helped him rationalize Jack's death, and yet, it would haunt him through the last years of his long life.

# DADDY'S RING

> Janet kept having the same recurring dream, which on this rare occasion was being influenced by the Dream Man. She kept dreaming of a ring, her daddy's wedding ring.

Janet had lost her father many years ago. Her mom had given what Janet thought was everything of his away as if there was no physical trace of him ever being alive except for a few recent photos and not many of those. It was as if her mother did not want to remember as remembering was too painful for her, so maybe she tried to pretend he didn't really exist.

Her mother had just passed away. Janet felt that they had now rejoined in that place where next-life decisions were made. She had plenty of personal items that belonged to her mother, so remembering the detail of life with her would be easy. However, she still longed for some personal item from her dad.

She never told her mom that for decades she periodically had dreams of her dad's plain, silver wedding ring but she never recalled seeing him wear it. She never brought the subject up to her mom fearing it would be too painful and bring back maybe some bad memories.

Since her mom's death, this dream began to increase in intensity and began occurring almost nightly at first, but after about a month, it was occurring every time she slept whether it be for a nap or for the night. It had gotten to the point she felt it would drive her crazy. And thanks to the Dream Man's efforts, that intensity would continue to increase until Janet got the message and her dream fulfilled. However, her dreams recently increased to include a man's brown wallet.

Janet woke up when this latest dream occurred and couldn't figure out its significance. After several occurrences of the dream, she had a particularly vivid occurrence of the wallet in her dream. In it she saw the initials JM, her dad's initials.

She immediately got up and began searching her mom's dresser, nightstands, every place in the house where such a wallet could be stored. However, she failed to find any trace of it. Then while having her morning coffee in the kitchen, she looked up and into the hallway and there she saw a trapdoor leading to what appeared to be the attic.

She immediately got a ladder, opened the trapdoor and climbed up to discover a light switch to the right of where she stood. She turned it on and to her amazement found a small, cardboard box. She excitedly opened it and found some old photos of her dad and mom. Under those photos she found the wallet she had dreamt about.

Janet was shaking with excitement and fumbled as she quickly pulled out the wallet and opened it. In the wallet was her daddy's silver wedding ring. At long last, she had her daddy's ring that she had dreamt about for so long. A ring that eventually would be worn by her future husband.

*Gerald L. Kovacich*

> The Dream Man although frustrated that it had taken so long for Janet to realize the meaning of her dreams, was happy that he was able to help another sentient being find a little happiness in this world of suffering.

# III

# THE END IS NEAR

# THE DEATH DREAM

As the Dream Man reached into his third century of life, he had his first and only dream. It was a dream of a stranger coming and the Dream Man's pending death. This dream made him realize that his time was near and soon he would die like all the other members of his clan before him, and return to the Void.

He was old and started to feel his 300-plus years on this earth. His knees were bad, so was his back, his hips, eyesight and seemed most joints constantly ached. He slept more often than not these days, comforted by the wolves who seemed to sense his pending death.

During one very deep sleep, he dreamt his one and only dream. He dreamt a stranger would approach, need his help and end up sharing life with him where the stranger would learn his ways and, learn to hear the voice in the Void. This confirmed to the Dream Man that yes, his life was indeed coming to an end. As he awoke, he smiled at the thought of it. The stranger did indeed arrive and spent many years learning from the Dream Man. Then one day the Dream Man smiled and then died.

He smiled and then died. He saw the brilliant white light, heard a voice that sounded familiar, one that he had heard deep in the recesses of his soul for all of his 300-plus years in his past life.

Death finally took the Dream Man at the appointed time.

So, at last the Dream Man got his wish, his replacement found and so he peacefully died in the mountain lair among his family, the wolves, where they dragged his body down to the valley to be taken by the vultures as was the clan's tradition.

# RETURN TO THE VOID

And the Voice said to him, "You have completed your life and have helped those in need of direction in their lives by interpreting their dreams for them and sending them on their Karma path or as you often wisely did, allowed them to continue in their current path. Now you can enter Nirvana where there is no suffering, no desires. You are released from rebirths, your past Karmas and are now in the state of perfect and eternal happiness."

"May I ask a question?" the Dream Man said.
"Yes," said the Voice.
"Now that I can enter Nirvana, does that mean that sentient beings no longer suffer?" he asked.
"No, only that you have done what was asked of you, so now you can rest," replied the Voice.
"Must I rest?"
"You have wanted to rest for over three hundred years and now after all that time of pleading for rest, you seem to say you are not ready to rest. Is that true?" asked the Voice.
He said, "It's just that resting seems selfish when so many sentient beings are suffering and there seems to be no end to their suffering. What can I do to help end their suffering?"

"You can return, but if you do, you must stay until all sentient beings' sufferings have ended. You may be reborn as a Bodhisattva, one that delays entering Nirvana out of compassion in order to save all suffering, sentient beings. You will be born with perfect knowledge. Since your last life was that of a male, in order to have perfect knowledge, you must be born a female."

The former Dream Man replied, "I don't mind. I just want to help end suffering."

The Voice answered, "You will return as Guanshiyin, which means 'observing the cries of the world'. The humans will call you Guanyin, Goddess of Mercy."

And with that, the Dream Man, now reincarnated as Guanyin, returned in spirit from the Void to help all sentient beings end their suffering and in doing so reach Nirvana. Her work continues to this day and based on our world of suffering, will continue for many thousands of years to come.

# FINAL COMMENTS

While hiking alone in the Western, wild country of Tibet, I became trapped in an early winter blizzard. I would have surely died if not for the Dream Man and his wolf pack who found me buried and near death in the snow. They took me back to the lair, his cave where I was to spend the next several decades learning from the Dream Man and the wolves.

They taught me about Life, Nature, the Tao. I learned to listen to the sounds of the Universe and learned that we are not alone. We are all connected throughout the Universe. Whether sentient being, or other lifeforms, we are connected and once we understand that, sense that, we should never fear being alone again and never fear death as there is no death of the soul.

As do all lifeforms, the Dream Man finally died. As he requested, his body was taken to the valley and given to the vultures, as was the custom of his clan for he too wanted his body to provide sustenance for another life-form.

As for me? Well, I guess I will continue the work of the Dream Man as my Karma had sent me there to replace him – at least those were the words of the Voice telling me to do so as I began to sense the dreams of others. And as the Dream Man said, I must listen to the Voice.

## About the Author

Gerald L. Kovacich has spent more than fifty years as a global traveler, poet, and observer of life, and he tries to live a life following the Buddhist philosophy of living a life of compassion, patience, charity, and love for all life forms.

He is also the author of more than seventeen books, primarily in the technology genre. Three of which have been translated into Japanese, Chinese, and Russian. His other books can be found on the usual websites for such things.

Gerald is a retired international consultant and lecturer currently residing on an island in Washington State, unless he is traveling in Asia and Europe, discovering more about people, places, and things.

Gerald's travels have taken him to many parts of the world, but mostly to countries of Asia where he learned their cultures, beliefs, languages and enjoyed their stories of Life.

Made in the USA
Monee, IL
25 June 2022